Matters of the Heart: The Healing God (4th Edition

Bethel Publishing House and Patience Sakutukwa

Published by Bethel Publishing House, 2024.

MATTERS OF THE HEART: THE HEALING GOD (4TH EDITION

First edition. December 25, 2024.

Copyright © 2024 Bethel Publishing House and Patience Sakutukwa.

ISBN: 978-1037023668

Written by Bethel Publishing House and Patience Sakutukwa.

Table of Contents

To the ever-present Healer, Jehovah Rapha, who stands sovereign over every diagnosis, chronic condition, and life-threatening illness, we acknowledge You as the ultimate source of healing regardless of the challenges we face. To all who are battling health struggles, to those enduring the weight of illnesses that threaten life itself. May you discover renewed strength in the boundless healing power of God, unshakable hope in His promises, and unending comfort in the truth that you are never alone in this journey. Even in pain, continue to declare the goodness of God, for He is not only the healer of the body but also of the soul. Trust in His faithfulness, for He is with you, every step of the way.

"LORD my God, I called to you for help, and you healed me."-Psalm 30:2 NIV

MATTERS OF
THE HEART

THE HEALING GOD
PATIENCE SAKUTUKWA

MATTERS OF
THE HEART
THE HEALING GOD
PATIENCE SAKUTUKWA

RESOURCES BY PATIENCE SAKUTUKWA
Matters of the Heart Edition 1
Matters of the Heart Edition 2
Matters of the Heart Edition 3
Matters of the Heart Study Bible
The Mentor & the mentee
God I Know NOTHING!
I Married a JEZEBEL
Kairos
Imago Dei

Bethel Publishing House

EPIGRAPHY

"LORD my God, I called to you for help, and you healed me."
-Psalm 30:2 NIV

DEDICATION

To the ever-present Healer, Jehovah Rapha, who stands sovereign over every diagnosis, chronic condition, and life-threatening illness, we acknowledge You as the ultimate source of healing regardless of the challenges we face. To all who are battling health struggles, to those enduring the weight of illnesses that threaten life itself. May you discover renewed strength in the boundless healing power of God, unshakable hope in His promises, and unending comfort in the truth that you are never alone in this journey.

Even in pain, continue to declare the goodness of God, for He is not only the healer of the body but also of the soul. Trust in His faithfulness, for He is with you, every step of the way.

FOREWORD

Life unfolds as a series of interconnected events, shaped by our decisions and their outcomes. While some circumstances fall within our sphere of control, others seem to overpower and guide us. Yet, in this unpredictable journey, one constant remains the heart. As the processor and the center of every experience, the heart holds the power to shape our responses, our resilience, and ultimately, our destiny. Too often, we neglect the sacred responsibility of reflecting on and stewarding the matters that flow through our hearts. Instead, we allow pain, anger, and disappointments to fester, unaware of their power to derail our lives. Yet, true victory the kind that transforms lives and brings lasting peace emerges only when we learn to master and direct the flow of our hearts. The greatest strength a person can attain is the mastery of their own heart.

A man or woman who governs their emotions, thoughts, and intentions is unshakable. They possess the ability to stand firm in the face of life's storms, unwavering in faith, wisdom, and purpose. In this remarkable book, *Matters of the Heart: The Healing God,* the author delves deeply into the challenges and triumphs of this heart journey. Through powerful reflections, transformative insights, and scripture-based guidance, readers will discover how to reclaim their emotional and spiritual well-being. This is more than just a book it is an invitation to examine the state of your heart and embark on the path to healing and restoration. It is a guide for anyone seeking to rise above the chaos of life and align their heart with God's truth and love. Prepare to be inspired, challenged, and empowered as you explore the profound truths contained within these pages. Master the matters of your heart, and you will master the course of your life.

Prophet Fungai Agabus Furati

PREFACE

There are moments in life when we are forced to confront the deepest wounds in our body and soul. For me, health challenges have been an ongoing battle that has tested my faith, strength, and spirit. Yet, through it all, I have clung to the goodness of God, who remains my healer and my refuge. This edition of Matters of the Heart is an intimate reflection on my journey through illness, pain, and God's healing grace.

As I share my story, I hope it speaks to those who are also walking through valleys of sickness and suffering. I have prayed for others to recover and witnessed their healing. But in the quiet moments of my own life, I often faced personal demons, life-threatening illnesses, and the lingering shame of afflictions that were passed to me due to sexual abuse.

Despite what the world may think or say, I have found my therapy in the healing God, the one who knows every part of me and still calls me His own. This book is a testament to His unwavering love and power to heal the most broken parts of us. It's a reminder that even in our pain, we can still declare His goodness. As you read through these pages, my prayer is that you, too, will find healing, hope, and renewed faith in the One who has been my strength when I had none.

INTRODUCTION

Have you ever prayed for someone to recover from sickness, witnessed their healing, only to return home and face your own life-threatening illness? Have you ever found yourself in one hospital after another, seeking answers and treatment, yet your health seems to deteriorate with each visit? Or perhaps, like me, you've felt the shame of suffering from chronic illnesses that were transmitted through acts of violence, like sexual abuse, only to have the world cast judgments without understanding the truth of your pain.

This is my story a journey of physical and emotional suffering, of facing the demons of illness and trauma, but ultimately finding solace in the healing God. Each chapter of this book explores the intersection of my health battles and the matters of my heart.

It is a vulnerable and painful narrative, but one that I share with the hope of offering comfort and healing to those who are suffering in silence. The truth is, healing doesn't always come the way we expect. Sometimes, it comes in the form of strength to endure, faith to keep going, or peace that surpasses understanding. Through every painful moment in my flesh, I kept declaring the goodness of God. And it is my hope that you will find the courage to do the same. This book is for you the broken, the suffering, the weary. May you find healing in these words, and may they point you to the God who heals.

Chapter 1

Matters of the Heart

Every book tells a story, but *Matters of the Heart* carries a legacy, a tapestry woven with threads of heartbreaks, disappointments, pain, hope, redemption, healing, deliverance, and the unwavering mercy of God. Spanning four editions and a Study Bible, each edition peels back a new layer of revelation and healing. What began as an exploration of relationships and the intricacies of human emotion has grown into a profound testament of God's relentless power to heal the brokenhearted. The journey began with the first edition, *Tested Wisdom for Relationships*. It opened doors to candid conversations about love, vulnerability, and the emotional toll of human connections. It resonated with anyone who had loved deeply and lost painfully.

The raw, unfiltered truth of those moments of standing on the precipice of heartbreak and looking over into the abyss struck a chord with many.

In the second edition, *Navigating Heartbreaks Through Shared Experiences*, readers were introduced to even more complex realities: the scars of addiction, the crushing weight of gender-based violence, the cold finality of divorce, and the delicate art of forgiveness. Here, the strength to move forward was illuminated, despite the lingering echoes of past hurts. It was a map for navigating the difficult terrain of brokenness and finding the courage to stand again.

The third edition, *Unmasking my Wounds so I can Heal* took us deeper into the heart of the author. Through the power of her own voice, the author unmasked the wounds that once lay hidden in the shadows for years.

In a raw act of catharsis, she poured out her soul on the page her hand a vessel for the pain of child abuse, betrayal, and the haunting lessons learned from mistakes. This edition explored the challenges of self-love, the struggle for inner peace amidst the storms of life, and the undeniable truth that healing begins from within.

And now, we come to the fourth edition: *The Healing God*. This edition transcends the surface of emotional pain, reaching into the very soul to uncover the transformative power of divine intervention. It is not just an invitation but a call to encounter the God who mends what seems beyond repair. Here, scars are not simply healed they are transformed into testimonies of grace. *"The wound is the place where the Light enters you,"* wrote Rumi, and truly, it is in the darkest of places where God's light shines the brightest.

This edition is for those who feel as though they have been broken beyond repair, for those who have suffered in silence, and for those who are longing to be whole again. The heart, as scripture reminds us, is the wellspring of life. Proverbs 4:23 warns us, *"Above all else, guard your heart, for everything you do flows from it."* It is the well from which our emotions, desires, and decisions flow, yet it is also the most fragile and vulnerable part of us. Guarding our hearts is not just a choice it is a command.

Matters of the Heart are universal. They touch everyone, regardless of age, gender, or background. Whether it is the joy of love or the agony of heartbreak, the heart becomes the battlefield. We wage wars of trust and betrayal, of hope and despair. And in the midst of it all, the heart bears the weight of our experiences, sometimes cracking under the pressure. But the beautiful truth is this: as much as the heart can suffer, it can also heal.

This book is not merely a continuation of the journey it is a deeper dive into the essence of healing. It acknowledges the pain life inflicts: betrayals, disappointments, and illness. Yet, it also offers a reminder that we are never alone in our suffering. The healing God walks beside us, His presence unwavering, ready to carry us through the darkest of nights.

Who is this healing God? He is the One who binds up the wounds of the brokenhearted (Psalm 147:3). He is the balm for emotional scars, the physician for physical ailments, and the healer of wounded souls. His healing is not just surface-deep. It reaches into the places no human intervention can touch into the core of who we are. In this edition, the focus shifts to the interconnectedness of the heart, soul, and body. Emotional pain often manifests physically through sleepless nights, stress-induced illnesses, and a weakened spirit.

Yet, healing also works the other way. As the soul finds peace in God's presence, the body begins to recover, and the heart becomes open once again to love, trust, and hope. The journey of healing is not linear it is a beautiful, messy process. It requires patience, perseverance, and faith. But most importantly, it requires the willingness to surrender to the healing God, the One who makes all things new.

Chapter 2

Venom in the Heart

Love, in its purest form, is meant to heal, uplift, and bind wounds. But when tainted by betrayal, it mutates into venom a poison that seeps into the soul, corroding the essence of who we are. This venom doesn't just wound the heart; it reshapes it with scars that even time struggles to mend. Betrayal shatters trust, extinguishes hope, and weaponizes the very dreams we once cherished. When the venom of heartbreak courses through the veins, the sanctuary of love transforms into a battlefield of anguish. One haunting question arises in such moments: *Where is God when it hurts?* Does He dwell in the silence of our unanswered prayers? Is He present in the tears that stain our pillows or the nights we spend clutching the fragments of our broken hearts?

As Rick Warren so poignantly writes, *"Your most profound and intimate experiences of worship will likely be in your darkest days when your heart is broken when you feel abandoned, when you're out of options when the pain is great, and you turn to God alone."*

In the fog of despair, it's easy to feel abandoned. But the truth is, God draws nearer in our brokenness. He whispers through the pain, promising restoration and gently reminding us that even the venom cannot separate us from His love. Betrayal demands a response, and its venom tempts us to lash out, build walls, and mirror the cruelty inflicted upon us. But how do we stay true to our values when vengeance seems so alluring?

Integrity is forged in the fires of adversity. It's not proven in moments of ease but in the face of betrayal, when bitterness beckons. Choosing forgiveness over retaliation, love over hate, and faith over despair is not an act of weakness but of profound strength.

When love transforms into venom, the heart retreats. It recoils, hesitant to open itself again, convinced that vulnerability will only invite more pain. How do we dare to love again? The answer lies in understanding that love is not defined by the failings of others. It is rooted in the unwavering, restorative love of God. Healing begins when we allow His love to wash over us, reminding us that even the most broken hearts can be made whole again.

After the betrayal, my apartment became my refuge a place to nurse my wounds and retreat from a world that felt hostile and alien. It was here, in the quiet of those walls, that I faced the venom's full weight. Every memory replayed like a cruel film, every hope turned sour casting long shadows over my days. The space, though cluttered and dim, mirrored the state of my heart. Yet, in this confinement, God began His work.

He met me in my solitude, gently sweeping away the bitterness and reminding me of His faithfulness. Cleaning that apartment became symbolic of the healing within me. The process of discarding the old, rearranging the necessary, and making space for something new paralleled the work God was doing in my heart.

Unbeknownst to me, the venom was not just spiritual and emotional it was physical. My health began to deteriorate, and by the time I realized it, I was on the brink of collapse. A visit to the doctor revealed that my kidneys were failing. For 48 harrowing hours, I was hospitalized, surrounded by the fragility of life. Psalm 91 came alive in those moments: *"He will cover you with his feathers, and under his wings, you will find refuge."*

Discharged at last, I returned home, overwhelmed by gratitude and sorrow. For weeks, I sobbed, pouring out my pain and thanksgiving to God. In the stillness of those tears, Psalm 30:1-3 became my anthem:

"I will extol thee, O Lord; for thou hast lifted me up, and hast not made my foes to rejoice over me. O Lord my God, I cried unto thee, and thou hast healed me."

Through those raw emotions, I encountered the depth of God's love a love that not only saved my body but began to restore my spirit.

Betrayal doesn't only linger in the mind; it manifests in the body. Stress-induced conditions, like "broken heart syndrome," are real, physically weakening the heart. Dr. Caroline Leaf notes, *"Unaddressed emotional pain becomes a breeding ground for physical illness."*

The venom of betrayal doesn't discriminate. Whether it stems from romantic relationships, friendships, or even professional partnerships, its symptoms are universal: isolation, anger, despair. Left unchecked, this pain festers, compounding over time and threatening to overwhelm. One night when I felt recovering, in the silence of my apartment, I opened my laptop.

Tears blurred my vision as I typed the question that had haunted me: *"God, must I endure this pain to write about it?"* As words poured onto the page, they became my outlet, prayer, and therapy. Writing hasn't just been about sharing a story; it has been my first step toward healing. With every sentence, I felt the venom lose its grip, replaced by God's gentle, transformative touch. Heartbreak is suffocating, but it doesn't have the final word. The healing process is slow and requires patience, surrender, and faith. My apartment, once a symbol of despair, became a sanctuary of hope a place where God turned my mourning into dancing, my pain into purpose. In the end, the venom did not define me. It refined me. Through betrayal, I learned resilience. Through heartbreak, I discovered the unyielding love of God. And through my pain, I found a purpose greater than myself to share this journey with you and to remind you that healing is possible.

So, as you turn these pages, may you find comfort and courage. May you come to know the healing God, not as a distant figure but as a personal Savior who walks with you through every valley, carrying you into the light of restoration.

Chapter 3

The Origins of a Disease

The human body, a marvel of divine creation, is both resilient and vulnerable. It is a vessel made for vitality and strength, yet it is susceptible to the forces of illness and suffering. Disease, whether arising from the tiniest microorganism or manifesting as a chronic condition, has puzzled humanity for generations. It's origins are complex, often intertwined with physical, environmental, spiritual, and emotional dimensions.

In my own life, I have faced the stark reality of illness. At one point, doctors gave me a bleak prognosis, and I struggled with chronic health challenges that left me grappling with questions about mortality and divine purpose. Despite the bleak prognosis from skilled doctors and the limits of scientific estimations, I continue to survive.

This resilience has revealed to me that health and healing are profoundly spiritual matters. How can one defy the precise calculations of medicine and science if not for the intervention of something greater than human understanding? Furthermore, the emotional and spiritual states of individuals such as unresolved bitterness, unforgiveness, or trauma can manifest physically, impacting health in profound ways.

Throughout history, people have sought to understand and combat disease. The very word *"disease"* originates from Middle English, denoting a state of discomfort or distress. Ancient societies, including those in biblical times, approached sickness through spiritual and practical means. In the Bible, Job's story illustrates suffering that is not tied to personal sin. Job 1:8–12 portrays his trial as a test of faith and endurance, ultimately revealing God's faithfulness in the face of unexplained illness.

Similarly, Jesus healed many during His ministry, demonstrating that some illnesses were opportunities to display God's power and compassion. John 9:1–3 recounts Jesus healing a man born blind, explaining that his condition was not a result of sin but existed *"that the works of God might be displayed in him."* The interplay of spiritual and emotional health with physical well-being is undeniable.

Proverbs 17:22 reminds us that *"A cheerful heart is a good medicine, but a crushed spirit dries up the bones."* Today, scientific studies affirm this truth, showing how stress, anxiety, and negative emotions can weaken the immune system and contribute to illness. Conversely, forgiveness, faith, and a positive outlook can play significant roles in recovery. Scriptures like Psalm 103:2–3 extol God's power to *"forgive all your sins and heal all your diseases,"* reflecting a holistic view of divine restoration.

The Spiritual Roots of Diseases

Many diseases have spiritual roots, and understanding how sickness enters and how to close the door is essential for healing. Sickness can enter through sin, trauma, emotional wounds, or disobedience to God's commands. James 5:16 tells us, *"The prayer of a righteous person is powerful and effective."*

The origins of disease trace back to the beginning of humanity's story. The Bible reveals that tragedy entered the world through the fall of Adam and Eve. Genesis 3 recounts their disobedience, which brought sin, pain, suffering and death into an existence that was originally designed to be perfect. However, not all illness stems directly from sin. Sometimes, it is the result of living in a world marred by brokenness. Other times, it reflects the consequences of lifestyle choices or environmental factors.

Poor diet, exposure to toxins, or neglect of physical well-being can contribute to sickness. Often, we hastily blame the devil or witches for our misfortunes, yet fail to acknowledge how we become our own adversaries, Indulging in unhealthy eating, reckless promiscuity, smoking or drinking and driving invites illness, accidents and countless other afflictions into our lives. In truth, our choices often sow the seeds of the very troubles we attribute to external forces.

Prayer, repentance, and faith can close the door to illness, inviting healing into our lives. Emotional wounds, unaddressed bitterness, and unresolved trauma can also contribute to physical ailments. The Bible warns against bitterness in Hebrews 12:15, which can cause spiritual and physical sickness. Unforgiveness and unresolved emotional pain can manifest in the body as physical illness, but through prayer and healing, the root causes can be addressed.

Healing is a multifaceted process that involves the body, soul, and spirit. While modern medicine provides invaluable tools and treatments, faith and prayer remain central to the believer's approach to recovery. James 5:14–15 instructs believers to call upon the elders of the church to pray for the sick, promising that *"the prayer of faith will save the sick person, and the Lord will raise him."* Prayer invites divine intervention, bringing comfort, hope, and restoration in ways that transcend human understanding. Modern medicine, too, has its place as an instrument of healing.

Just as Naaman was healed of leprosy through Elisha's guidance (2 Kings 5:10–14). Naaman, whose name means "pleasantness" or "graciousness," was a man of great honor and reputation. As the commander of the Syrian army, he was a symbol of authority and strategic brilliance, beloved by his king and respected by his people.

His leadership and military achievements brought victory and security to his nation, and he held a position of unparalleled influence. Despite his many merits his valor in battle, his strategic genius, and his commanding presence Naaman was a man in crisis. Beneath his armor of success lay a body ravaged by leprosy, a chronic and disfiguring disease that threatened to strip him of his dignity and legacy. Leprosy, a term historically used to describe a variety of chronic skin conditions, was a source of physical, emotional, and social devastation.

In Naaman's time, it was viewed not just as a disease but as a symbol of uncleanness and exclusion. The causes of leprosy, now known as Hansen's disease, are linked to a bacterial infection (*Mycobacterium leprae*), which spreads through prolonged close contact with an infected individual. The disease primarily affects the skin, nerves, and mucous membranes, leading to numbness, deformities, and severe complications if left untreated. While modern medicine has developed effective treatments using multidrug therapy, in ancient times, no cure existed, making leprosy a lifelong affliction for most. Naaman's leprosy was more than a physical ailment it was a spiritual and emotional weight. For a man accustomed to command, strength, and admiration, his condition symbolized vulnerability and the fragility of even the greatest among us. Yet, in his sickness, Naaman's story also became one of divine healing and redemption, revealing the power of God to restore what seemed hopelessly lost. Through the guidance of a young servant girl and his encounter with the prophet Elisha, Naaman dipped himself in the Jordan River seven times, obeying the divine instruction. His skin was restored, "like that of a young boy," and he emerged healed and humbled, acknowledging the God of Israel as the true source of power and life. Naaman's journey reflects the reality faced by many of the world's great leaders and public figures today.

Across the globe, individuals in positions of influence pastors, presidents, and other prominent icons often grapple with chronic illnesses while bearing the weight of their responsibilities. Their battles with illness reveal the universal vulnerability of humanity, showing that no amount of power, wealth, or fame can insulate one from the trials of disease. Globally, the prevalence of chronic illnesses among leaders and high-profile individuals is a growing concern, especially as stress and demanding schedules take a significant toll on their health. According to the World Health Organization (WHO), more than 20% of adults over the age of 40 are living with a chronic condition, which includes a substantial proportion of those in leadership positions who operate in high-stress environments. These leaders often face an increased risk of stress-related health issues, such as heart disease, hypertension, and diabetes, which disproportionately affect them due to the intense pressures of their roles.

Public figures are particularly vulnerable, often delaying medical care in favor of fulfilling their responsibilities, despite the serious nature of their conditions. The personal stories of iconic leaders like Nelson Mandela and Franklin D. Roosevelt exemplify this resilience. Mandela, who fought against tuberculosis while imprisoned.

Frank Delano Roosevelt (FDR) (1882-1945), the 32nd President who led the United States while dealing with the paralysis caused by polio, exemplifies the extraordinary ability of leaders to persevere through debilitating health challenges. He is the only president to serve four terms, though he passed away early in his fourth term. (1933-1945). Their experiences serve as a testament to the strength required to carry on, despite chronic illness, and the unique pressures that high-profile individuals face in managing their health while maintaining public duties.

In ministry, pastors and spiritual leaders are no exception. A 2023 survey by the Barna Group found that 40% of pastors report dealing with chronic illnesses such as hypertension, diabetes, and autoimmune disorders. Despite their physical limitations, many continue to lead congregations and inspire faith, becoming living testaments to God's sustaining grace.

A Healing God in a Broken World

Naaman's story is a reminder that healing is not bound by human limitations. In a world where leaders and icons are as vulnerable as the people they serve, his miraculous recovery points to the power of God to intervene in the midst of crisis. While medical advancements have brought hope and healing to millions, there are still moments when only divine intervention can address the deepest wounds of body and soul.

For leaders like Naaman, who face both the pressures of leadership and the pain of chronic illness, healing is more than a physical restoration it is a spiritual awakening. Naaman's transformation from a proud commander to a humble servant of God shows us that healing is not just about the body but about the soul's surrender to the Creator. As we reflect on his journey, we are reminded that God's healing power is available to all, transcending time, status, and circumstance.

Whether it is a modern pastor leading a congregation despite an autoimmune disease or a president making decisions while battling cancer, their stories echo the truth of Naaman's experience: the healing God still works miracles, and His grace is sufficient even in our weakest moments. God often uses doctors, nurses, and treatments to bring about restoration. However, recovery is not always immediate.

Some experience miraculous healing, while others walk a gradual journey of restoration that tests and refines their character. Illness, while challenging, is not the end of the story. It is a reminder of human frailty and a call to rely on God, the ultimate source of life and health. Whether faced with chronic conditions, sudden illnesses, or genetic challenges, believers can trust in God's sovereignty and grace. Even when healing does not come as expected, Romans 8:28 reassures us that *all things work together for good to those who love God.*

Closing the Door to Sickness

To heal, we must address the spiritual root of the illness. Repentance, prayer, and seeking forgiveness open the door for God's healing power to flow freely into our lives. As we close the doors to sin and emotional pain, we open ourselves to God's restoration. So learn to view sickness and health through a lens of faith, understanding, and hope.

It challenges us to see illness not as a punishment but as an opportunity to draw closer to God and to witness His power at work in our lives. Through faith, science, and community, we can navigate the complexities of disease with courage and trust in the One who holds our lives in His hands.

Chapter 4

The Refining Fire of Pain

Pain speaks a universal language that transcends cultures, races, and economic boundaries. It is an uninvited guest, capable of shattering the strongest hearts and challenging even the firmest faith. Yet, pain is more than just suffering it is a profound teacher, a silent transformer, and a relentless revealer. The very word "pain," derived from the Latin *poena* (punishment) and the Greek *poinē* (payment or penalty), underscores its dual nature: a reminder of hardship with purpose. In the tapestry of life, pain becomes the thread that refines, tests, and prepares us for something greater than ourselves. Pain strikes unexpectedly, often leaving us unprepared. Its manifestations are as varied as human experience itself, marking our hearts and souls. Betrayal is one form of pain that lingers like poison.

When a loved one such as a spouse betrays our trust, the wound is not just in the act but in destroying the foundation of trust, leaving deep scars that can take years to heal. Corruption also carries a heavy burden. When those in power misuse their influence for selfish gain, they destroy systems and erode countless individuals' hopes. The pain is not just in the injustice but in the helplessness of knowing power has been abused.

Rejection, too, is a painful face of life. Whether it's a parent distancing themselves emotionally or friends abandoning us, rejection creates a deep loneliness, making us question our worth. This wound often runs far beneath the surface, leaving lasting, invisible scars.

Loss, especially through death or separation, alters everything. The world feels incomplete, and our sense of reality becomes distorted. Grief is an indescribable pain understood only through experience, where each breath becomes heavier and each day longer.

Unmet expectations serve as painful reminders of our limitations. The dreams we work so tirelessly to build only to see them crumble create a pain that feels like defeat. It's not failure itself that stings most, but the belief that we were so close, yet not enough. Isolation, one of the cruelest forms of pain, often comes when we are left to face struggles alone. The weight of abandonment when others choose to walk away becomes unbearable, deepening our sense of loneliness.

Finally, false accusations can pierce the heart like a sharp sting. Being condemned for crimes we did not commit doubles the agony. It's a pain that not only questions our worth but also forces us to battle on multiple fronts internally, emotionally, and externally. Pain reveals the vulnerability of the human spirit. It forces us to confront our weaknesses, fears, and brokenness. But within these trials lies the potential for growth, healing, and deeper understanding of ourselves and the world around us.

If we allow pain to shape us, rather than defeat us, it can lead to profound transformation. Each experience of pain provokes deep questions: *Why me? Why now? Will this ever end?* Even the prophet Jeremiah cried, *"Why is my pain unending and my wound grievous and incurable?"* (Jeremiah 15:18). Pain is inevitable. It arrives without warning, altering the course of our lives. Though its presence is often unbearable, pain possesses a transformative force that can either break us or build us, shaping our character and capacity to endure. Without faith, despair threatens to overwhelm us; with it, even the darkest valleys become navigable. Job, despite his immense loss, exemplified unwavering trust in God's sovereignty: "Though He slay me, yet will I hope in Him" (Job 13:15). Romans 8:28 assures us that *"in all things, God works for the good of those who love Him."* Although we may not see the purpose of our pain immediately, faith sustains us, reminding us that God is weaving our trials into His redemptive plan.

Choosing Healing

Pain offers a choice: to let it break us or build us. Healing begins with acknowledgment facing our wounds without denial. It requires forgiveness not for the sake of offenders but for our liberation. Isaiah

61:3 promises "a crown of beauty instead of ashes," a divine exchange that transforms despair into joy. Healing also calls for surrender laying our burdens at God's feet, trusting Him to bring restoration. Left unchecked, pain hardens hearts and sows bitterness. But when entrusted to God, it refines and redeems. Every trial carries within it seeds of purpose. Joseph's suffering in slavery and imprisonment prepared him for leadership and reconciliation. Reflecting on his journey, he told his brothers, *"You intended to harm me, but God intended it for good"* (Genesis 50:20). Our pain equips us to comfort others and bear witness to God's faithfulness.

It turns scars into stories of triumph, reminding us that no suffering is wasted in God's hands. Losing my parents remains one of my life's deepest wounds. My father's absence left an emptiness that I felt keenly as I grew. My mother's passing compounded that loss, transforming holidays once filled with joy into painful reminders of what was gone. Yet, through these dark seasons, pain became my teacher. It humbled me, deepened my faith, and taught me resilience. Pain has shown me its dual nature: a thief of joy and a catalyst for growth. It has refined my character, enabling me to minister to others with empathy and understanding. Though the scars remain, they testify not to defeat, but to the strength that emerges when we allow God to use our suffering for His glory. In pain's crucible, I found purpose. It taught me that even the most shattering moments can birth new life, new hope, and new beginnings. And so, I press on, knowing that God is always near, crafting beauty from the ashes of my trials.

Chapter 5

Suffering

"Many families are in severe pain, resulting in suffering suffering from life-threatening illnesses, bitterness, heart attacks, and high blood pressure. But God does not want us to suffer." *(Psalm 34:19: "The righteous person may have many troubles, but the Lord delivers him from them all.")* Suffering often feels like an unrelenting storm, one that sweeps through lives with no warning, leaving destruction in its wake. For many, suffering is a constant companion looming, inescapable, and unforgiving. It wears different faces, appearing as the physical agony of chronic illness, the emotional pain of heartbreak, the spiritual dryness of feeling distant from God, or the economic hardship of poverty and injustice.

Yet, despite its many guises, suffering shares one cruel trait: it lingers, demanding to be felt and acknowledged. Picture the anguish of a mother praying beside her child's hospital bed, hoping for a miracle that seems so far away. Imagine the silent torment of a man whose heart is heavy with depression, unable to find the strength to speak of his pain. Envision the quiet grief of an elderly widow, her days filled with echoes of laughter that have long since faded. These are but glimpses of suffering reach, and in each of these scenarios lies the universal cry: *Why must I endure this?*

The question of suffering's purpose and duration often haunts those walking through life's valleys. It can feel like a prison sentence without a clear end, leaving many to wonder why healing seems delayed. The answer is not always clear, but one thing is certain: suffering is not God's desire for us. He is not the author of our pain but the Redeemer of it.

As Psalm 34:19 assures us, though the righteous may face many troubles, the Lord promises to deliver them all. Suffering is not always easy to recognize, especially when it does not take a physical form. It can linger in the shadows of the mind, as bitterness takes root and grows.

Unforgiveness, for example, is a silent suffering that chains us to the very source of our pain. Like an untreated wound, it festers, poisoning every part of our being. Bitterness and anger prolong suffering, locking the heart in a cycle of resentment that is hard to break.

Spiritual suffering, too, is often overlooked but can be just as debilitating. When we feel disconnected from God, the weight of our trials becomes unbearable, as though we are carrying the burden alone. This disconnection can sometimes result from our own withdrawal when shame, doubt, or pride keeps us from seeking His presence.

Even isolation, whether chosen or imposed, magnifies suffering. In times of pain, many withdraw from their communities, either out of fear of judgment or the mistaken belief that they must carry their burdens alone. Yet God calls us into fellowship with others, knowing that through shared love and support, the load becomes lighter.

A negative mindset can also perpetuate suffering. Words of defeat, hopelessness, and despair turn the mind into a prison. When we speak life over our circumstances and meditate on God's promises, we begin to see glimpses of light piercing the darkness. But this transformation requires trust trust in God's timing, trust in His plans, and trust in His ability to redeem even the most painful seasons of our lives.

While suffering can feel purposeless, it is often through these trials that God refines us, draws us closer to Him, and prepares us for a greater calling. Romans 8:28 reminds us that in all things, God works for the good of those who love Him. This does not mean the pain will vanish overnight or that healing will always come in the way we expect. Instead, it means that even in our deepest suffering, God is at work, shaping our hearts and revealing His glory.

Consider the story of Joseph, whose suffering seemed endless. Betrayed by his brothers, sold into slavery, falsely accused, and imprisoned, Joseph could have easily given up. But through every trial,

God was preparing him for a greater purpose to save a nation and reconcile his family. Similarly, our suffering is not wasted. Every tear, every sleepless night, and every unanswered prayer is seen by the One who promises to wipe away all tears and make all things new.

God's ultimate plan is to bring us to a place where there is no more suffering, no more pain, and no more tears. Revelation 21:4 paints a picture of this promise, reminding us that while suffering is temporary, God's love and redemption are eternal. Until that day, we are called to lean on Him, trusting that He is walking with us, even when the path is hard to see.

If you are suffering today, take heart. God sees your pain, hears your cries, and holds you close. Your suffering is not the end of your story. It is a chapter painful, yes, but not without purpose. Place your burdens at His feet, and let Him carry what you cannot. As you wait for healing, remember that you are not alone. The same God who walked with Joseph, who bore the cross for our sins, and who defeated death itself walks with you now, offering hope, strength, and the promise of a brighter tomorrow.

Chapter 6

The Healing God

Healing is a process that transcends mere physical recovery. It is about restoration in mind, body, and spirit. The word "healing" comes from the Old English word *hælan*, meaning "to make whole" or "to restore to health." In biblical terms, healing is deeply intertwined with the concept of wholeness and restoration. The origin of healing is not only seen in the physical sense but also in the emotional, mental, and spiritual realms. **To heal** (as understood in Hebrew and Greek) means to "make complete," or "to bring into a state of soundness." In the Bible, God is revealed as the ultimate Healer. **Jehovah-Rapha**, meaning "The Lord Who Heals," is one of God's titles, emphasizing His power to restore His people physically, emotionally, and spiritually.

This name appears in the Old Testament, in Exodus 15:26: *"He said, 'If you listen carefully to the Lord your God and do what is right in His eyes, if you pay attention to His commands and keep all His decrees, I will not bring upon you any of the diseases I brought upon the Egyptians, for I am the Lord, who heals you.'"* God's healing is not limited to the physical, and it's not just about the absence of pain. It is the restoration of peace, joy, and hope sometimes in places that seem beyond repair. Healing in the Bible is also depicted through miracles performed by Jesus, from curing the sick to raising the dead, as recorded throughout the Gospels. In Matthew 4:24, it is written, *"News about Him spread all over Syria, and people brought to Him all who were ill with various diseases, those suffering severe pain, the demon-possessed, those having seizures, and the paralyzed; and He healed them."*

The Journey of Healing

Healing is not a destination, but a journey a journey that is as unique as the person experiencing it. For some, the road may be straight and smooth, while for others, it may wind with detours, obstacles, and unexplainable miracles. This chapter is not written from a place of having all the answers. Rather, it is a reflection of my own journey a story that is still unfolding, marked by both pain and miraculous healing.

Growing up, I became familiar with the cold, sterile walls of hospitals, with doctors telling me that I had "limited time" and "chronic conditions" that would require "lifelong management." These phrases, once terrifying, became background noise yet, they still carried weight over my life, as I was constantly reminded of what my condition might mean for my future. However, it was during this time that I encountered God in ways that defy explanation.

A Silent Suffering

In my teenage years, I faced challenges that I had never expected. Abuse both verbal and sexual from those who were supposed to love and protect me left scars that not even the best doctors could heal. The wounds left by the betrayal were deep, and the shame of it all left me questioning my worth. But even in the darkest moments, God's presence was near. Psalm 34:18 reminds us, *"The Lord is close to the brokenhearted and saves those who are crushed in spirit."* It was in these times of anguish that I began to experience His healing touch, one that did not come immediately but began to unfold slowly.

There were many days when I felt as though my body had betrayed me. Every diagnosis came like a wave, with each one more terrifying than the last. The doctor's words spoken with cold finality reminded me of my mortality. "There is no cure," they said. "You will have to live with this for the rest of your life."

Yet, even as I attended the funerals of the very doctors who had predicted my end, I realized a profound truth: **Man's time is not God's time.** His plans for us are not confined to the limits of human understanding.

Miracles in the Midst of Pain

Despite the prognosis, I saw God's hand at work. I experienced healing that could not be explained by science or medicine. Tests that once showed grim results suddenly turned favorable, and surgeries that carried great risks resulted in miraculous recoveries. Exodus 14:14 became my anthem: *"The Lord will fight for you; you need only to be still."* This scripture didn't promise that the journey would be easy, but it reminded me to trust even in the midst of uncertainty. Healing, I realized, is a partnership between God and us. It is about aligning our faith with His will, even when we don't understand what's happening.

The Role of Doctors & Therapists

God's healing is not always instantaneous. Sometimes, He uses doctors, therapists, psychologists, and other professionals to aid in the restoration process. While God is the ultimate Healer, He works through the skills and wisdom He gives to others. It is important to remember that healing encompasses more than just spiritual recovery it involves the body, the mind, and the emotions. Whether through surgery, counseling, or therapy, God's healing power often flows through those He has equipped to help us along the way.

Self-Love as Part of the Healing Process

One of the most important aspects of healing is learning to love ourselves. Self-love is not about vanity or selfishness; it is about accepting who we are flaws and all. It is about understanding that we are worthy of love and forgiveness, even when we feel undeserving.

True healing begins when we stop condemning ourselves for past mistakes and accept ourselves as God sees us. We learn to recognize our worth, despite the scars of our past. Through self-love, we give ourselves the space to heal. We acknowledge the pain of our experiences, but we also recognize our strengths. God created us with a purpose, and even when we feel broken, we are still a vessel for His work. As Joyce Meyer writes in her book *Beauty for Ashes*, "God does not waste any pain. He uses it to bring healing and restoration to us so that we can help others."

Self-love is about acknowledging our humanity our need for healing and allowing ourselves to go through the process without judgment. As Dr. Anita Johnson so beautifully writes in *The Garden Within*, "In the depths of your soul, there is a garden that only you can tend. It is here that healing begins, and it is from here that you will grow."

The Power of God in Healing

Healing is not a quick fix or a one-time event it is a process, a journey of restoration. God's healing power is not just a solution to our physical ailments, but a comprehensive transformation of who we are. It is the healing of the brokenhearted, the restoration of our joy, and the reawakening of our spirit. In Isaiah 53:5, we read, *"But He was pierced for our transgressions, He was crushed for our iniquities; the punishment that brought us peace was on Him, and by His wounds, we are healed."*

The cross of Jesus is the ultimate symbol of this healing a reminder that through His suffering, we have been restored. Healing requires patience. It requires trust. And it requires a willingness to surrender our pain to the Healer. In doing so, we not only find healing for ourselves, but we become a source of healing for others. We become vessels of God's grace, sharing His love and restoration with a broken world.

Chapter 7

Types of Healing

Healing is a journey, and understanding its different types helps us navigate through life's struggles more effectively. In this chapter, we'll explore the various forms of healing physical, emotional, mental, and spiritual, and how they align with the types of professionals or "doctors" one might need to consult for each form. Healing is not just about physical recovery but also about restoring wholeness to every aspect of our being. Physical healing, one of the most tangible and widely recognized forms of recovery, involves the restoration of the body from ailments such as illness, injury, or disease. Just as people seek out medical professionals for treatment, divine healing often complements these interventions.

Whether through medications, surgeries, or therapies, God works through human knowledge and resources to bring health to the body. Yet, ultimately, He remains the supreme Healer, and the process of recovery, though sometimes immediate, can also be a journey of faith and resilience.

Scripture affirms this truth in *Exodus 15:26*, where God promises health to those who follow His commands: "I am the Lord, who heals you." This promise is demonstrated in the story of Hezekiah, who faced a dire prognosis yet turned to God in prayer. His healing was a combination of divine intervention and practical remedies, showing that God's power is often manifested through accessible means (*Isaiah 38:21*).

Similarly, emotional healing addresses the deep wounds left by rejection, loss, betrayal, and disappointment. These scars, though invisible, require tender care and intentional efforts toward recovery.

Therapists, counselors, and supportive communities play a pivotal role, but emotional healing often finds its foundation in the comforting presence of God. The psalmist reminds us in *Psalm 34:18*, "The Lord is close to the brokenhearted and saves those who are crushed in spirit."

Joseph's life offers a profound example. Despite the betrayal of his brothers, the injustice of slavery, and wrongful accusations, Joseph found healing through God's providence. This restoration not only mended his emotional wounds but also elevated him to a position of authority and reconciliation (*Genesis 45:4-8*). His journey illustrates that emotional healing is both a process and a testament to God's faithfulness. Whether physical or emotional, healing in all its forms points back to the enduring care of a loving God, who restores and renews in His time and wisdom.

Healing from emotional pain involves the painful process of confronting past wounds, forgiving others, and allowing God's love and grace to fill the voids left behind. This is not always an immediate healing but one that requires time, reflection, and surrender to God. Mental healing focuses on the intricate workings of the mind, addressing thoughts, beliefs, mental illnesses, and unhealthy patterns of thinking. In the same way that individuals seek guidance from psychiatrists or psychologists for mental health concerns, the process of mental healing often requires professional help. Yet, it is equally important to align one's thoughts with the truth of God's Word and allow the Holy Spirit to renew the mind.

Paul captures this transformative journey in *Romans 12:2*, urging believers, "Do not conform to the pattern of this world, but be transformed by the renewing of your mind." This renewal brings clarity, enabling one to discern God's good and perfect will.

The story of Job illustrates this beautifully. Amid the torment of loss and suffering, Job experienced profound mental and emotional anguish. But through an intimate encounter with God, his mind was restored as he refocused on God's sovereignty and faithfulness (*Job 42:5-6*).

Mental healing is a process of breaking free from destructive thought patterns, lies, and mental chains that can trap us in anxiety, depression, or confusion. By allowing Christ to renew our minds, we step into a space of peace, joy, and clarity that only He can provide.

Equally vital is the need for spiritual healing a profound restoration of one's relationship with God and the healing of the soul. This type of healing requires confession, repentance, and a heartfelt desire to draw closer to God. The Prodigal Son's journey in *Luke 15:11-32* offers a poignant example.

After straying from his father, the son's return symbolizes how spiritual healing begins with humility and an acknowledgment of our need for God. As his father welcomed him with open arms, so too does God receive us when we return after periods of wandering or sin.

Spiritual healing is deeply rooted in Christ's redemptive work, as prophesied in *Isaiah 53:5*: "He was pierced for our transgressions, crushed for our iniquities; the punishment that brought us peace was on Him, and by His wounds we are healed." This type of healing calls for an ongoing surrender of pride and self-reliance, inviting us to live in alignment with God's will. Through this process, the soul finds peace, forgiveness, and the fullness of a reconciled relationship with the Creator.

Together, mental and spiritual healing reveal a God who is intimately involved in the restoration of every aspect of our being, guiding us from brokenness into wholeness through His grace and power.

The Healing Process

Healing is a **process** and not a single event. Just as doctors may need multiple visits and treatments to restore physical health, emotional, mental, and spiritual healing often requires time and consistent effort. Healing begins with acknowledgment a moment of clarity when we recognize that something within us needs attention, whether it be emotional, mental, or spiritual. Just as we visit a doctor for physical ailments, we must confront our inner wounds to set the healing process in motion. This self-awareness opens the door to restoration.

Seeking help follows naturally, as healing often requires guidance. Whether we turn to a therapist, a spiritual mentor, or immerse ourselves in the Word of God, the act of seeking allows God to work through human instruments. These helpers become vessels for His grace, offering wisdom and support as we navigate our struggles.

True healing, however, requires surrender. It is only by entrusting the process to God that we can experience full restoration. This surrender is an act of faith, where we let go of control and trust in His divine plan, even when the path is unclear or the pain persists. Patience becomes our companion in this journey. Healing, like physical recovery, is rarely instantaneous. It demands perseverance, especially when feels slow progress or setbacks occur. But with patience, each small step forward becomes a victory, reinforcing our resolve to keep moving.

Ultimately, the destination of healing is restoration and transformation. It is here that we become whole not just in body, but in mind and spirit. Through this process, we emerge stronger, more resilient, and more attuned to God's presence in our lives. Healing doesn't just repair what was broken; it reshapes us, creating a version of ourselves that is both renewed and empowered.

Healing & the Role of Professionals

God is the ultimate healer, but He also works through human professionals. Doctors, therapists, counselors, and spiritual leaders are important instruments in the healing process. We are called to respect and value their contributions while recognizing that the true source of all healing comes from God. Healing is a journey, not a single, instantaneous event. Much like how physical recovery often requires multiple visits to a doctor or prolonged treatment, the restoration of emotional, mental, and spiritual health demands time, intentionality, and consistent effort. It begins with acknowledging the need for healing, an essential step that mirrors the moment we admit something is physically wrong and seek medical attention. Recognizing emotional, mental, or spiritual wounds requires humility and courage, as it is the first step toward transformation.

The journey continues with seeking help, whether through medical professionals, therapists, spiritual mentors, or the wisdom of God's Word. Healing often involves collaboration; God, the ultimate healer, frequently works through human hands to restore what is broken. Doctors, counselors, and spiritual guides are vital instruments in this process, each contributing unique expertise and insight. Their work serves as a reminder that God's care reaches us in tangible ways through the people and resources He provides.

Surrender and trust form the foundation of true healing. Just as a patient must trust their physician's expertise, we must surrender our healing process to God, trusting Him to guide us toward full restoration. This trust becomes our anchor, particularly when healing feels slow or challenging. Patience and perseverance are indispensable in this journey, as wounds of all kinds physical, emotional, mental, and spiritual require time to heal. Even when progress seems imperceptible, the act of holding onto faith sustains us. Ultimately, healing leads to restoration and transformation. It is not merely about returning to a previous state of well-being but about emerging renewed, stronger, and more deeply attuned to God's presence. Through healing, we become whole again, experiencing a transformation that equips us with resilience and a greater appreciation of life's beauty. The role of professionals in this process cannot be overstated. In physical healing, doctors, nurses, and other healthcare workers act as God's hands, restoring health and alleviating suffering. For emotional and mental healing, therapists and counselors offer the tools, support, and guidance needed to navigate pain and rebuild. Spiritual healing is often facilitated by pastors, mentors, and spiritual leaders who draw upon the Word of God to offer prayer, discipleship, and wisdom. Each of these individuals plays a significant part, yet the ultimate source of healing remains the divine power of God.

In every step of this journey, healing is a testament to the intricate interplay between divine intervention and human effort, reminding us that God's hand is always present, whether through miraculous acts or the skilled work of professionals dedicated to our restoration. Healing is a holistic process involving every aspect of our being body, mind, and spirit. Understanding the different types of healing and recognizing the professionals who assist in each process helps us appreciate the complexity of God's restorative work in our lives. As we seek healing, we must remember that God is the ultimate healer, and He uses a variety of methods, including medical intervention, counseling, and spiritual guidance, to restore us to wholeness. In every step, we must surrender our hearts to Him, trust in His perfect timing, and be open to the ways He will restore and heal us. Healing is not a destination but a continuous journey of transformation one that brings us closer to the heart of God.

Chapter 8

Doctor Jesus Christ

In the world of medicine, there are many specialists, renowned for their ability to heal, to cure, and to restore health. However, there is only one who is the Master Physician, the Ultimate Healer, the one who not only understands the human body but also the soul, mind, and spirit. His name is Doctor Jesus Christ, and His clinic operates beyond the confines of earthly hospitals, offering healing that transcends all human limitations.

Imagine a place where every ailment, every wound, every disease is addressed with perfect precision and understanding. The surgery room of *Doctor Jesus* is not a sterile, cold room with bright fluorescent lights, but a sacred space where divine love flows like an eternal river, cleansing, healing, and restoring.

Here, there are no mistakes, malpractice, or missed diagnoses. Jesus, the Great Physician, knows every detail of every person's body, mind, and heart, and He operates with flawless perfection. The operating table of this sacred surgery room is not made of steel or cold metal, but of grace and mercy. The instruments He uses are not of this world but are crafted in the heavens: the sword of the Word, the balm of His presence, and the anointing oil of the Holy Spirit. Every surgery is performed with the gentleness of a loving Father, yet with the power of the Creator who made every cell, every bone, and every heartbeat.

His Prescription: Faith, Prayer, & Trust

What does Doctor Jesus prescribe to His patients? It is not a bottle of pills or a course of treatment like any earthly doctor. His prescription is simple, yet profound: **Faith**, **Prayer**, and **Trust** in Him.

These divine prescriptions, when followed with obedience, bring miraculous healing that cannot be found in any medical journal or clinic. Jesus did not just heal the body He healed the soul. His prescriptions not only alleviated physical pain but also brought peace to the troubled hearts of those who came to Him. He didn't hand out prescriptions that required refills, for the healing He provides is complete and eternal. When His touch comes, there is no sickness, no disease, and no pain that can withstand the power of His love.

The Rate of His Effectiveness

What sets Doctor Jesus apart from any earthly healer is the effectiveness of His healing. His success rate is flawless 100%. No matter the sickness, no matter the time or place, when Jesus enters the scene, healing begins. His healings are instantaneous for some, progressive for others, and for a few, He allows the process of waiting to deepen their faith.

But the true miracle is not just in the physical healing; it is in the spiritual restoration. Jesus' healing is holistic body, soul, and spirit. His treatment extends beyond the body, reaching the deepest parts of a person, restoring the broken, mending the lost, and giving hope to the hopeless.

Why Some Patients Don't Recover

Despite His miraculous power and perfect healing record, not every patient who comes to Doctor Jesus experiences healing in the way they expect. Some are healed instantly; others experience a process of healing, and some may face the hardest of trials, experiencing suffering and even death. Why? Jesus does not fail, but sometimes, His healing comes in ways we do not understand. Some patients may not receive the immediate relief they seek, and others may face prolonged suffering. But the divine wisdom of the Healer goes beyond our comprehension.

Perhaps, in these moments, He is using the trial to refine our faith, to draw us closer to Him, or to teach us lessons we can only learn through suffering. Sometimes, like the Apostle Paul who pleaded with the Lord three times to take away his "thorn in the flesh," we may not understand why healing doesn't come as we expect. But we must trust that even in these moments, Doctor Jesus is working whether in our bodies or in our hearts.

Patients Who Live & Are Cured

Throughout the Gospels, we see many who came to Doctor Jesus and were healed in ways beyond imagination. The woman with the issue of blood, who pressed through the crowd just to touch the hem of His garment and was instantly healed (Matthew 9:20-22). The blind man, whose sight was restored with a simple touch (Mark 8:22-26). The paralyzed man, was lowered through the roof by his friends, who stood up and walked after Jesus declared him healed (Luke 5:17-26).

These stories are not just historical accounts they are declarations of the power of Jesus Christ to heal. These testimonies stand as a reminder to us today that Doctor Jesus is still in the business of healing. His clinic is open 24/7, and His healing is available to all who believe.

Declarations of His Healing Power

I declare, in the name of Jesus, that healing is not just a possibility it is a promise. I declare that His healing touch is available to anyone who calls upon His name in faith, no matter the severity of their sickness. To the broken-hearted, I speak healing over your life. Jesus, the balm of Gilead, is here to mend every wound and restore your heart. His love reaches the deepest pain and brings peace where sorrow has lingered. To those enduring suffering in their bodies, I declare the healing power of Christ upon you. By His stripes, you are healed. His mighty hand is ready to move in your life, restoring health and wholeness as you trust in Him.

To those spiritually weary and drained, may the Lord breathe new life into your soul. Jesus, whose grace is always sufficient, will renew your strength and restore your spirit. Lean on Him, for He is your source of revival and unshakable hope.

Testimonies of Doctor Jesus

The pages of the Bible and the testimonies of countless believers testify to the miraculous workings of Doctor Jesus. From the healing of lepers to the raising of the dead, the evidence is clear: there is no illness too great, no problem too vast, and no soul too lost for His healing touch. There are countless stories of people who were healed by Jesus' power, and even today, there are those who have experienced healing miracles in His name. These testimonies continue to echo through the halls of time, affirming that Doctor Jesus Christ is the same yesterday, today, and forever (Hebrews 13:8).

Bragging on Doctor Jesus

There is no earthly physician who can compare to the healing power of Doctor Jesus. He does not just treat symptoms. He cures the very root cause. He does not simply ease pain. He transforms lives. His clinic is open to all, and His rates are beyond affordable, for He has already paid the price.

We can confidently brag on Doctor Jesus, not because of what we have seen Him do for us, but because of who He is the Great Physician, the Healer of souls, the Restorer of bodies. We are His living testimonies, His evidence of divine intervention, and His proof that He still heals today. Doctor Jesus, we honor you. We trust in your healing touch, and we give You all the glory for the miracles You continue to perform. You are our Healer, and there is none like you!

Chapter 9

The Power of Forgiveness & Healing

Forgiveness is not only essential for spiritual growth but also plays a profound role in our physical and emotional healing. The Bible makes it clear that forgiving others is key to receiving forgiveness and healing from God. In Matthew 6:14-15, Jesus says, *"For if you forgive other people when they sin against you, your heavenly Father will also forgive you."* This divine exchange links forgiveness directly with healing, emphasizing that unforgiveness can be a barrier to God's healing power in our lives. Medical studies also support this biblical principle, showing that unforgiveness can increase the risk of stress-related conditions such as heart disease, high blood pressure, and depression.

In The Healing Power of Forgiveness, Dr. Archibald Hart suggests that emotional wounds from unresolved forgiveness can manifest as chronic illnesses. He also points out that forgiveness allows the body to heal, as it releases negative emotions and reduces stress. Forgiveness allows the spirit to heal, leading to peace in the mind and, eventually, restoration in the body. As we forgive, we align ourselves with God's will for our lives and free ourselves from emotional and physical burdens.

Chapter 10

The Mind-Body Connection

The connection between the mind and body is profound, with modern science beginning to support what Scripture has long declared that our thoughts, emotions, and spiritual well-being directly impact our physical health. Proverbs 4:23 teaches, *"Above all else, guard your heart, for everything you do flows from it."* Our heart, or mind, is the seat of our thoughts and emotions, which in turn can affect our physical well-being. Mental health conditions like anxiety and depression have been linked to higher rates of chronic illnesses such as heart disease, diabetes, and even cancer.

In her book *The Power of the Subconscious Mind*, Dr. Joseph Murphy discusses how the subconscious mind influences physical health.

By focusing on healing and positive thoughts, individuals can improve their health, as they shift their mindsets to align with God's will. In Philippians 4:6-7, Paul assures us that God's peace *"will guard your hearts and minds in Christ Jesus."* This peace goes beyond understanding and is essential in healing. By cultivating this peace through prayer, meditation, and faith, we not only heal emotionally but also physically, as peace promotes overall health and reduces stress.

Chapter 11

The Healing Power of Worship

Worship invites God's presence into our lives, and where His presence dwells, healing flows. Scripture provides many examples of how worship led to divine healing and breakthroughs. Psalm 22:3 says, *"But you are holy, enthroned on the praises of Israel."* Worship enthrones God in our lives and invites His healing presence. When we face sickness, worshiping God brings us into a space where healing can occur. As we focus on God's power and majesty, our bodies and spirits align with His purpose for healing. Author Don Moen in his book The Healing Power of Praise and Worship highlights the transformational effect of worship on our mental and physical state.

Worship is a powerful tool that can provide relief, restore peace, and bring about physical healing. Experiencing God's Healing Presence through Worship. In the presence of God, healing occurs not only in our hearts but also in our bodies. The Bible speaks of God's glory filling the temple in 2 Chronicles 5:13-14, showing that worship brings God's presence and glory, where healing flows abundantly.

Chapter 12

Breaking Generational Curses

Curses, whether believed to be divine retribution, ancestral retribution, or the result of spiritual forces, have permeated human history for millennia. Across different cultures, religions, and societies, the concept of a curse carries profound significance an unseen force that brings misfortune, suffering, or death. But what exactly is a curse, and how does it operate in our lives? More importantly, how can the healing power of God, Jehovah Rapha, help us break free from the curse that holds us captive?

In this chapter, we will explore the nature of curses, their origins, and their manifestation in cultures worldwide. We will examine the phenomenon of generational curses, and delve into the methods used across different traditions to break such curses.

Finally, we will understand how Jehovah Rapha, the God who heals, offers a way of escape from these forces of darkness and brings true healing and freedom.

What Are Curses and Their Origins?

A curse, in its simplest definition, is a proclamation or act that invokes harm, misfortune, or divine punishment on an individual or group. Curses are often seen as a tool of divine justice, employed either as a response to a violation of sacred laws or as a form of vengeance. In ancient times, both the Egyptians and Greeks viewed curses as a powerful tool of gods or spirits used to exact punishment for transgressions. Ancient Egyptian curses, for instance, were inscribed on tombs to warn off tomb robbers, with promises of death or misfortune upon those who dared to disturb the dead.

In Judeo-Christian tradition, curses are often associated with sin and disobedience. In the Bible, curses are seen as consequences of human rebellion against God. For example, Deuteronomy 28 details a list of curses that would come upon the Israelites for disobedience, including sickness, famine, and defeat in battle. These curses were seen as an integral part of the covenantal relationship between God and His people. Similarly, in the Old Testament, the concept of curses was also tied to the idea of holiness and maintaining purity in the community.

James H. Charlesworth, in his work *The Old Testament Pseudepigrapha* (1983), notes that ancient cultures universally believed in curses as mechanisms for controlling divine order and enforcing morality. He writes, "Curses, whether through divine or human agency, were seen as corrective measures aimed at restoring moral or cosmic order" (Charlesworth, 1983).

The Cycle of Sin and Suffering

One of the most troubling aspects of curses is when they extend across generations. Generational curses, also known as ancestral or family curses, are believed to result from sins or patterns of dysfunction that are passed down from one generation to another. These curses manifest in various ways physical illness, mental disorders, poverty, relational dysfunction, and emotional trauma. For many, the experience of generational curses feels like an unending cycle of suffering that is inherited from ancestors, often with no clear way out.

The Bible provides clear references to the concept of generational curses. In Exodus 20:5-6, God declares, *"You shall not bow down to them or worship them; for I, the Lord your God, am a jealous God, punishing the children for the sin of the parents to the third and fourth generations of those who hate me."*

This passage underscores the impact of sin, not just on the individual but on subsequent generations. Yet, there is hope embedded in the biblical narrative. In contrast to the curse, God's mercy and grace are extended to *"a thousand generations of those who love me and keep my commandments"* (Exodus 20:6). **Walter Brueggemann** (2002), in his book *Theology of the Old Testament*, emphasizes that while God's judgment is passed down, His mercy and covenant love are far more potent, offering a path of healing even for those caught in the grip of generational sin.

The Role of Rituals in Curses & Healing

Rituals associated with curses are found in almost every culture. A ritual is defined as a set of actions performed according to a prescribed order, often for spiritual or religious purposes. In many cultures, rituals for invoking or breaking curses are seen as a means of restoring balance to the spiritual or cosmic order.

These rituals vary widely, depending on the culture, belief system, and understanding of spiritual forces. For example, **African Traditional Religions** have long relied on rituals to address curses, particularly those passed down through generations. According to **John Mbiti** (1969), a scholar of African religions, rituals in these contexts are performed by religious leaders or elders who invoke ancestral spirits to address the issue of a curse. In some cases, sacrifices of animals or offerings of food are made to appease the spirits and seek protection or healing. The **"cleansing" rituals** are meant to rid the individual or community of the spiritual stain left by the curse.

In **Hinduism**, rituals to remove curses often involve the recitation of mantras, prayers, or specific sacrifices to deities believed to possess the power to break spiritual chains.

Stephen G. Alter (2001), a scholar of South Asian religions, explains that these rituals serve to "purge the soul of negativity and reset the spiritual balance," aligning the individual with divine order. However, while these rituals may provide temporary relief, **Christian theology** teaches that true freedom from curses comes not through ritualistic appeasement but through the redemptive work of Jesus Christ. The Bible teaches that curses are broken through repentance and the power of Christ's sacrifice, not through ritual alone. **Timothy Keller**, in his book *Walking with God through Pain and Suffering* (2013), writes, "Christ's work on the cross is the ultimate antidote to the curse of sin.

His life, death, and resurrection break the power of every curse, from the curse of the law to the curses that plague us in our lives today."

Breaking Free through Christ

The ultimate solution to the problem of curses lies not in human rituals, but in God's divine intervention through Jesus Christ. Galatians 3:13 reminds us that *"Christ redeemed us from the curse of the law by becoming a curse for us."* The power of generational curses is broken through Christ's sacrifice on the cross. We no longer have to live under the shadow of sin's consequences. Through repentance, prayer, and faith in Christ, we can break free from the cycle of generational curses and experience healing in every area of our lives.

The healing power of Jehovah Rapha is essential in this process. **Jehovah Rapha** means "The Lord who Heals," and He is the ultimate healer of physical, emotional, mental, and spiritual wounds. He is not limited by the depth of the curse or the history of sin in our lives. His power to restore is immeasurable.

J. I. Packer, in his theological work *Knowing God* (1973), writes, "Jehovah Rapha is not merely a God who heals physically but one who heals the soul healing the emotional wounds caused by generational sins and curses." When we align ourselves with Christ and embrace His redemptive power, we are set free from the curses that have haunted our families and our futures.

The Power of Prayer and Repentance

Breaking free from generational curses requires us to acknowledge the presence of these curses and confront them in the light of Christ's sacrifice. Prayer and repentance are essential in this process. In **James 5:16**, we are instructed to *"confess your sins to each other and pray for each other so that you may be healed."* Prayer is a tool of spiritual warfare that allows us to break the strongholds of sin and the spiritual forces that hold us captive.

Repentance is the first step. **David Platt**, in his book *Radical* (2010), asserts that "true repentance is not just a change of behavior but a complete transformation of the heart." When we confess our sins and turn away from the iniquities that have plagued our family line, we are aligning ourselves with God's plan for healing and restoration.

Embracing Freedom & Restoration

Generational curses are real, but they do not have to define our lives. Through the redemptive work of Christ, and the healing power of Jehovah Rapha, we can break free from the spiritual bondage that has held us captive. This is not a freedom that is won through ritual or effort alone, but through grace the grace that is available to all who believe in Christ and seek His healing touch. The power of curses may be deeply embedded in the fabric of our lives, but the power of God is greater.

Jehovah Rapha, the God who heals, is available to heal us not just physically, but emotionally, mentally, and spiritually. Let us step into His freedom and walk in the healing that only He can provide. This topic is part of my book on titled *"Not Cursed but Blessed."* where I delve deeper in curses and blessings.

Chapter 13

Faith and Healing

Faith, derived from the Greek word *pistis* in the New Testament, signifies trust, belief, and assurance in God's character and promises. In Hebrew, the root word for faith, *emunah*, denotes steadfastness and reliability, reflecting the consistent nature of God as depicted in the Old Testament. Faith originates from a divine gift, as described in Ephesians 2:8, which states, *"For by grace you have been saved through faith, and this is not your own doing; it is the gift of God."* Faith is foundational to healing and addressing matters of the heart. In biblical narratives, faith often serves as the bridge connecting human frailty to divine intervention. For example, in Mark 5:34, Jesus tells the woman healed of her prolonged ailment, *"Daughter, your faith has made you well."*

Here, faith is portrayed not just as belief in the possibility of healing but as a profound trust in God's will and power. Faith also plays a critical role in the emotional and spiritual healing necessary for overcoming heartbreak or unresolved pain. Dr. Timothy Keller, in *Walking with God through Pain and Suffering*, explores how faith anchors believers during life's storms, providing a foundation for resilience and restoration. By trusting in God's promises, individuals can navigate the emotional complexities of brokenness and experience healing that transcends human understanding.

The origin of faith ties directly to its application in matters of the heart, where trust in God's providence, character, and redemptive power enables healing. Romans 10:17 reminds us *that "faith comes from hearing, and hearing through the word of Christ."*

Immersing oneself in God's Word strengthens this faith, making it a vital instrument for overcoming emotional wounds and restoring spiritual wholeness. Faith, rooted in God's enduring nature, becomes the bedrock for confronting heartbreak, generational curses, and the physical and emotional scars of life. Its divine origin ensures that it is not merely a human endeavor but a heavenly tool for achieving the transformative healing God offers.

Faith is a key ingredient in receiving healing. Without faith, it is impossible to please God or receive His healing power. Jesus often linked healing with faith. Faith opens the door to the miraculous. When we trust God for healing, we activate His power to transform our situation. Healing is not just a physical process but a spiritual one, where our trust in God unlocks the door to His intervention.

Dr. Randy Clark, in his book *The Healing Breakthrough*, explains that faith is the trigger that activates God's power for healing. Faith is not simply believing God can heal but believing He will heal you, standing firm on His Word. Walking by faith means trusting that God's healing is available to us today. Romans 8:11 tells us that *"the Spirit of him who raised Jesus from the dead is living in you."* The same power that raised Jesus lives in every believer, providing the power to walk in divine health. Faith plays a multifaceted role in the process of healing, interacting seamlessly with spiritual gifts such as the gift of faith, the gifts of healing, and the working of miracles.

Together, these gifts operate as an intricate symphony of divine power, manifesting God's glory in the lives of believers. The gift of faith stands out as a supernatural ability to believe in God's promises beyond human reasoning.

It is not ordinary faith but an extraordinary endowment that empowers believers to trust God for the impossible. Dr. Derek Prince, in *Faith to Live By*, describes this gift as a profound conviction that aligns our will with God's purposes, enabling the miraculous to unfold.

When coupled with the gifts of healing and working of miracles, the gift of faith serves as a catalyst that initiates divine intervention. The gifts of healing operate as a channel through which God's power addresses physical, emotional, and spiritual ailments. Unlike natural remedies, these gifts are manifestations of God's supernatural grace. Dr. Randy

Clark, in *The Healing Breakthrough*, emphasizes that faith acts as a conduit for activating these gifts. He highlights that when believers pray with unwavering confidence, healing becomes not just a possibility but a reality. The working of miracles takes this interplay a step further by demonstrating God's omnipotence in extraordinary ways.

Miracles often challenge natural laws, proving that God's power transcends human limitations. In the story of Elijah, as narrated in 1 Kings 17, the resurrection of the widow's son exemplifies how faith and the working of miracles collaborate.

Elijah's unwavering trust in God enabled a supernatural act that restored life and strengthened the widow's faith. Faith has always been pivotal in the body of Christ. The Bible is replete with examples of individuals whose faith ushered in healing and miracles. The centurion in Matthew 8:5–13 demonstrated such great faith that Jesus marveled, declaring, "Go! Let it be done just as you believed it would." His servant was healed that very moment. Similarly, the persistent faith of the Canaanite woman in Matthew 15:21–28 resulted in her daughter's deliverance from demonic oppression.

Beyond biblical accounts, historical figures in the church exemplify the transformative power of faith. Smith Wigglesworth, a renowned evangelist, attributed countless healings and miracles to unshakable faith in God's promises. His life and ministry epitomize how faith, coupled with the Holy Spirit's gifts, can bring about divine intervention.

Faith's role extends beyond individual experiences to influence the collective body of Christ. Dr. Caroline Leaf, in *Switch On Your Brain*, underscores that faith positively affects mental and emotional well-being. By renewing the mind with God's Word, believers can align their thoughts with divine truths, fostering an environment where healing flourishes. As we walk by faith, we are called to trust that the same Spirit who raised Christ from the dead resides within us, empowering us to live victoriously.

Romans 8:11 reminds us that this resurrection power is not a relic of the past but an ever-present reality for those who believe. Faith, when activated, transforms our lives, bringing healing, restoration, and the miraculous into our daily walk with God. This chapter highlights that faith is not passive but an active force that bridges the human and the divine.

It invites us to participate in God's redemptive work, aligning our hearts and minds with His purposes to experience the fullness of His healing power. Whether through individual acts of belief or the collective faith of the body of Christ, faith remains the cornerstone of experiencing God's transformative grace.

Chapter 14

The Hope of Healing & the Future Cure

While the journey of healing can be long and challenging, there is hope in the promise of complete healing. The Bible offers us an eternal hope for healing in the life to come, where sickness, pain, and death will be no more. In Revelation 21:4, it is written, "He will wipe every tear from their eyes. There will be no more death or mourning or crying or pain, for the old order of things has passed away." This ultimate healing gives us hope for the future, even as we face the realities of sickness and disease on earth. Though we may not always experience complete healing in this life, we can rest in the assurance that God's perfect healing will be realized in eternity. As we wait for the ultimate healing, we can trust that God is still at work in our lives, providing partial healing, comfort, and hope as we look forward to the day when all will be restored.

CASE STUDIES

Chronic Diseases & Pandemics

Throughout history, mankind has been beset by afflictions that rob individuals of their health, their happiness, and often their very lives. Chronic illnesses and pandemics have plagued human existence, causing suffering that is both visible and invisible, stretching across generations and continents. These diseases are not only physical but also emotional and spiritual burdens that deeply impact individuals, families, and societies. From the rise of infectious diseases like the Black Death in the 14th century to the ongoing struggle with chronic conditions like cancer, diabetes, and HIV/AIDS, the human race has fought a relentless battle for survival, healing, and hope.

In every century, there has been a defining disease that has captured the world's attention, often leaving a trail of devastation in its wake. In the 14th century, the Black Death wiped out an estimated 30% to 60% of Europe's population, spreading fear, despair, and sorrow. People watched as their loved ones succumbed to an invisible killer, and entire villages were wiped off the map. This pandemic not only took lives but also shattered communities, leaving people questioning the nature of life, death, and God's purpose in the midst of suffering.

Fast forward to the 20th and 21st centuries, and we face new, equally destructive battles. Cancer, with its many forms and relentless progression, has become a modern-day affliction, stealing the health, dreams, and sometimes even the hope of individuals and families. Every year, millions are diagnosed, and many lose their lives to this disease.

Families are torn apart as they watch their loved ones endure debilitating treatments and the slow progression of the disease. The emotional toll of cancer is often just as heavy as the physical, as families grapple with grief, fear, and the loss of control over their futures.

HIV/AIDS, first identified in the early 1980s, has similarly left a profound mark on the global community. Sub-Saharan Africa has borne the heaviest burden, with millions of people infected, often facing stigma, rejection, and isolation. In many communities, the disease has robbed entire generations, leaving children orphaned and families torn apart. Despite the medical advancements in antiretroviral therapy, the emotional and spiritual scars of HIV/AIDS remain, with individuals continuing to struggle with fear, loneliness, and the heavy weight of societal judgment.

And then, as the world was beginning to grasp the gravity of these ongoing crises, the COVID-19 pandemic emerged, striking with unprecedented speed and ferocity. This new global crisis has affected every corner of the world, bringing with it not only the threat of death but also a deep emotional, physical, and spiritual toll. The virus has left millions sick and dead, and entire economies and societies have been disrupted. In addition to the physical suffering, the pandemic has caused a rise in mental health challenges, with individuals facing isolation, anxiety, and fear as they watch their loved ones battle an unseen enemy. Healthcare systems, already stretched thin from dealing with other diseases, have been further strained, and the emotional toll on frontline workers has been immense. People have lost loved ones, lost jobs, lost a sense of normalcy and in many ways, lost hope.

These chronic illnesses and pandemics are not mere statistics they represent real people, families, and communities. The suffering they bring is not just the pain of the body but also the anguish of the heart. They rob individuals of their dreams, their vitality, and sometimes even their dignity. The trauma is far-reaching, impacting mental health, relationships, and spiritual well-being. But amidst this suffering, one thing remains certain: God is a healer.

In the face of pain, illness, and loss, the healing power of God has been witnessed in countless lives. The journey of healing is not always immediate or without difficulty, but through faith, prayer, medical advances, and divine intervention, many have found restoration. The stories of those who have battled chronic illnesses and pandemics are filled with both tragedy and triumph, suffering and healing, grief and hope.

Through these case studies, we will explore how chronic illnesses like HIV/AIDS and cancer, and global crises such as the COVID-19 pandemic, have affected the world—and how the Healing God has shown up to restore, heal, and provide hope.

As we delve into these case studies, we will examine the origins of these diseases, the profound impact they have had on individuals and societies, and the ways in which modern medicine and spiritual healing have worked hand in hand. We will also look forward to a future where healing continues to be a possibility whether through medical advancements or through divine intervention and explore the hope that remains for those still suffering.

Case Study 1

HIV/AIDS Versus the Healing God

HIV/AIDS is one of the most persistent and challenging global health crises, having significantly impacted millions of lives since its discovery in the early 1980s. It is a disease that carries both physical suffering and emotional anguish, as well as societal stigma and spiritual challenges. The pandemic has affected millions worldwide, with particular devastation in regions like sub-Saharan Africa. This case study will explore the origins of HIV/AIDS, the suffering it has caused, and the ways in which God has intervened to bring healing to individuals living with the disease. It will also highlight the medical progress made over the years and how faith and spiritual healing play a significant role in managing the disease.

Origins & Spread of HIV/AIDS

HIV (Human Immunodeficiency Virus) was identified in the early 1980s and is transmitted primarily through blood, semen, vaginal fluids, and breast milk. It weakens the immune system, making the body susceptible to infections and certain cancers, leading to AIDS (Acquired Immunodeficiency Syndrome), the final stage of the disease. Initially, the disease was most prevalent among certain high-risk groups, including men who have sex with men, intravenous drug users, and sex workers. However, HIV/AIDS has since become a global epidemic, affecting people of all ages, genders, and backgrounds. Sub-Saharan Africa remains the region most affected by HIV/AIDS, with over 70% of the world's HIV-positive population living in this area. Countries like South Africa, Zimbabwe, and Kenya have some of the highest rates of HIV prevalence, with millions of people living with the disease.

In these regions, HIV/AIDS has been a major driver of death and suffering, exacerbating poverty, societal instability, and the burden on healthcare systems. The physical suffering caused by HIV/AIDS is multi-faceted. As the virus attacks the immune system, individuals experience a range of debilitating symptoms, including weight loss, chronic diarrhea, fever, fatigue, and skin infections. As the disease progresses to AIDS, people are at greater risk for life-threatening infections like pneumonia, tuberculosis, and opportunistic infections. These infections can lead to severe pain and hospitalizations, which contribute to both physical and emotional distress. Emotionally, individuals diagnosed with HIV/AIDS often experience feelings of fear, shame, isolation, and depression. Stigma and discrimination surrounding the disease are widespread, particularly in countries with high levels of ignorance about HIV transmission.

This stigma can lead to the rejection of people living with HIV, further compounding their emotional suffering. Over the years, significant progress has been made in managing HIV/AIDS through medical advancements. In the early years of the epidemic, there were no effective treatments, and individuals with HIV quickly progressed to AIDS and often died prematurely. However, the introduction of antiretroviral therapy (ART) in the 1990s revolutionized HIV treatment. ART involves a combination of medications that suppress the replication of the virus, allowing people living with HIV to maintain a higher quality of life and live longer.

When taken consistently, ART can reduce the viral load to undetectable levels, meaning the virus cannot be transmitted to others, a phenomenon known as "undetectable = untransmutable" (U=U).

In countries with high HIV prevalence, ART has been provided through government programs and international aid organizations, such as the Global Fund and PEPFAR (President's Emergency Plan for AIDS Relief). ART is free or heavily subsidized in many sub-Saharan African countries, but challenges remain in reaching remote areas and ensuring adherence to the lifelong treatment regimen. Side effects of ART, such as nausea, headaches, and fatigue, are common, but the benefits of suppressing the virus far outweigh the risks.

While ART has been a breakthrough in treating HIV, it does not address the emotional and spiritual pain that often accompanies the disease. For many individuals living with HIV/AIDS, faith plays a critical role in coping with the suffering. Spiritual healing can take many forms, from prayer and scripture reading to support groups within religious communities.

Testimonies from people living with HIV often reveal the transformative power of faith in their journey. One testimony from a woman in South Africa shared how, after being diagnosed with HIV, she turned to her church for support. She found comfort in prayer and the reassurance that God's love for her remained steadfast despite her illness. Through the prayers of others and her own faith, she was able to cope with the emotional weight of the disease and maintain hope for the future.

The Healing God is experienced through the emotional healing that faith offers. In addition, some people have reported miraculous physical healing through prayer and spiritual intervention. While not everyone experiences a physical cure, the emotional and spiritual healing through faith in God has been profound for many.

Modern Generation & HIV/AIDS

The modern generation has seen significant advances in HIV/AIDS treatment and prevention. The introduction of PrEP (pre-exposure prophylaxis), a medication that prevents HIV transmission, has opened new possibilities for preventing the spread of HIV, particularly for at-risk populations. The younger generation is also more educated about HIV transmission, reducing stigma and promoting safer sexual practices. However, despite medical progress, there is still a need for continued education, compassion, and support for those living with HIV/AIDS. The modern generation must not forget the role of faith in the healing process, both emotionally and spiritually. God continues to show up as a healer, offering hope and comfort to those who suffer.

Case Study 2

COVID-19 Versus the Healing God

The COVID-19 pandemic, which began in late 2019, has been one of the most significant global health crises of the 21st century. It has impacted every aspect of life physically, emotionally, spiritually, and economically. With millions of people infected and millions of lives lost, COVID-19 has left a trail of suffering that is still being felt worldwide. This case study will explore the origins of COVID-19, the global impact of the pandemic, and how God's healing power has been manifested during this time of crisis. COVID-19 is caused by the novel coronavirus, SARS-CoV-2, which was first identified in Wuhan, China, in December 2019. The virus spread rapidly across the globe, leading the World Health Organization (WHO) to declare a global pandemic in March 2020.

COVID-19 is primarily transmitted through respiratory droplets, and its symptoms range from mild to severe, including fever, cough, fatigue, difficulty breathing, and loss of taste or smell. In severe cases, COVID-19 can lead to pneumonia, organ failure, and death, particularly in individuals with underlying health conditions. The pandemic led to widespread lockdowns, social distancing measures, and travel restrictions. Healthcare systems in many countries were overwhelmed with the surge of cases, and the global economy was severely impacted by the necessary measures to control the virus's spread. The physical suffering caused by COVID-19 has been devastating.

Millions have contracted the virus, and millions have died. Those who survive often face long-term symptoms known as "long COVID," which can include chronic fatigue, brain fog, muscle pain, and respiratory problems.

Healthcare workers, who have been on the front lines, have experienced physical exhaustion and emotional burnout due to the overwhelming number of patients. Emotionally, the pandemic has caused widespread anxiety, fear, and grief. The loss of loved ones, the uncertainty of the future, and the isolation caused by social distancing have led to significant mental health challenges.

Many people have struggled with depression and anxiety, and the spiritual impact has been profound. For many, the question of why such suffering has occurred has led to spiritual crises, where faith has been tested. The pandemic disproportionately affected individuals with chronic illnesses, such as diabetes, hypertension, and respiratory conditions. People with these pre-existing conditions were at higher risk of severe illness and death from COVID-19.

In addition, the pandemic exposed and exacerbated health disparities in low-income communities, particularly in sub-Saharan Africa and Latin America, where access to healthcare resources was limited. While the pandemic caused immense suffering, it also provided opportunities for healing through faith and community. Churches and religious organizations quickly adapted to the crisis by moving services online, offering virtual prayer meetings, and providing emotional support to those in need.

Testimonies of God's healing power were shared, as individuals found comfort and strength through their faith, even in the midst of crisis. For example, a woman in New York City who contracted COVID-19 shared how, while in the hospital on a ventilator, she experienced a profound spiritual awakening. Through the power of prayer, she found peace and felt God's presence in a way that brought her comfort and strength to fight the illness.

She eventually recovered, and her testimony became a source of hope for others battling the virus. In response to the pandemic, scientists and healthcare workers around the world worked tirelessly to develop vaccines to combat COVID-19. The rapid development of vaccines has been a monumental achievement in the fight against the virus, offering hope for a return to normalcy. At the same time, spiritual healing has played a critical role in helping individuals cope with the emotional and psychological toll of the pandemic. God's healing presence has been felt in countless stories of recovery, hope, and peace. As we look toward the future, there is hope not only for physical healing through medical advancements but also for spiritual restoration as people return to their faith. The COVID-19 pandemic has been a global tragedy, but it has also highlighted the importance of faith and healing.

As we move forward, we must continue to rely on both medical science and spiritual healing, knowing that God is always present to heal, restore, and provide hope in the face

CONCLUSION

The heart is the epicenter of human existence, the reservoir from which emotions, thoughts, and actions spring forth. Every person, at some point, grapples with matters of the heart—love and loss, hope and despair, pain and healing. These experiences define our humanity and reflect our deepest vulnerabilities. Yet, in its vulnerability, the heart holds unparalleled strength when anchored in God's truth and love.

Guarding the heart is not merely a suggestion but a divine imperative. When Proverbs declares, *"Above all else, guard your heart, for everything you do flows from it"* (Proverbs 4:23), it illuminates the heart's role as the wellspring of life. To guard our hearts means to cultivate discernment, to consciously filter what we allow into our innermost being.

Whether through the relationships we nurture, the media we consume, or the thoughts we entertain, every influence shapes the condition of our hearts. Discernment is an act of love, a commitment to protect what is sacred.

Healing and guarding the heart are deeply intertwined. True healing begins when we surrender the matters of our hearts to the Healing God, Jehovah Rapha. Whether the pain stems from rejection, betrayal, or disappointment, God offers balm for the wounded heart. Through His Word, prayer, and the transformative power of His Spirit, brokenness is mended, and scars become testimonies of grace. The process of healing is not always immediate; it often mirrors the slow, steady recovery of physical wounds. Yet, in the waiting, God shapes and strengthens, drawing us closer to His purpose.

Forgiveness is perhaps one of the most potent ways to guard the heart. Bitterness and resentment corrode the soul, blocking the flow of joy and peace.

Forgiveness is not an endorsement of wrongdoing but a release a decision to entrust justice to God and to free ourselves from the chains of anger. In forgiving, we reflect the grace we have received, allowing God's love to take root and flourish.

Gratitude transforms the heart into fertile soil for healing and growth. Choosing to focus on God's goodness amidst pain shifts our perspective, reminding us of His faithfulness. It strengthens our resolve and guards us against despair. Gratitude is an act of worship that elevates the heart above its struggles, aligning it with the eternal hope found in Christ. The matters of the heart are not isolated incidents but a lifelong journey. Each challenge, each victory, and each moment of healing draws us deeper into the mystery of God's love.

As we walk this journey, let us remember to guard our hearts with vigilance, not by building walls of fear but by creating sanctuaries of trust where God's presence dwells. His promises are the shield that protects and the hope that sustains.

May this book serve as a reminder of the Healing God who sees every wound and hears every silent cry. May it inspire you to guard your heart with all diligence, trusting in the One who heals, restores, and renews. And may your heart, in all its matters, find peace and wholeness in the arms of the Creator.

As we come to the end of this transformative journey, may this book serve as a beacon of hope, a source of inspiration, and a reminder of the healing power of God in every aspect of life. Healing is not merely an event but a continuous process that intertwines our faith, perseverance, and divine grace.

Whether physical, emotional, mental, or spiritual, healing is an invitation to trust in Jehovah Rapha, the God who heals, and to walk boldly in the assurance of His promises.

Let us not forget that healing often transcends our individual experiences, calling us to be vessels of comfort and hope to others. Just as Christ restored broken lives, we, too, are equipped to extend love, prayer, and encouragement to those around us. In doing so, we become living testimonies of God's redemptive power, shining His light into a world in need of restoration.

May this book ignite a deeper trust in God, strengthen your faith, and empower you to embrace the beauty of healing, even in the midst of challenges. Go forth, healed and healing, as a witness to the One who makes all things new.

BIBLIOGRAPHY

Books and Articles

1. Erikson, Millard J. *Christian Theology*. Grand Rapids: Baker Academic, 1998.

2. Keller, Timothy. *Walking with God through Pain and Suffering*. New York: Riverhead Books, 2013.

3. Leaf, Caroline. *Switch On Your Brain: The Key to Peak Happiness, Thinking, and Health*. Baker Books, 2013.

4. Leaf, Caroline. *Cleaning Up Your Mental Mess: 5 Simple, Scientifically Proven Steps to Reduce Anxiety, Stress, and Toxic Thinking*. Baker Books, 2021.

5. Phillips, Anita. *The Garden Within: Where the War with Your Emotions Ends and Your Most Powerful Life Begins*. Harper Inspire, 2023.

6. Wright, N. T. *Surprised by Hope: Rethinking Heaven, the Resurrection, and the Mission of the Church*. San Francisco: Harper One, 2008.

7. Charlesworth, James H. *The Old Testament Pseudepigrapha*. Doubleday, 1983.

8. Brueggemann, Walter. *Theology of the Old Testament*. Fortress Press, 2002.

9. Platt, David. *Radical: Taking Back Your Faith from the American Dream*. Multnomah, 2010.

10. Packer, J. I. *Knowing God*. Hodder & Stoughton, 1973.

11. Alter, Stephen G. *The Sacred and the Profane: The Rise of Modern Rituals in Hinduism*. Princeton University Press, 2001.

12. Mbiti, John. *African Religions and Philosophy*. Heinemann, 1969.

References
Case Studies

1. Nelson Mandela: Analysis of his perseverance through tuberculosis during imprisonment, as referenced in *Long Walk to Freedom* by Nelson Mandela.

2. Franklin D. Roosevelt: Insights into his leadership despite living with polio,

as referenced in *FDR* by Jean Edward Smith.

3. Joseph's Story: A biblical narrative from Genesis 37-50, illustrating emotional and spiritual healing through God's providence.

Scripture References

- Exodus 15:26
- Psalm 34:18
- Romans 12:2
- Isaiah 53:5
- Luke 15:11-32
- Job 42:5-6

Acknowledged Medical and Therapeutic Insights

- World Health Organization (WHO). "Chronic Illness Statistics and Insights."
- American Psychological Association (APA). Resources on Emotional and Mental Health.

ACKNOWLEDGEMENTS

I extend my deepest gratitude to Jehovah Rapha, the Healing God, for His grace and inspiration throughout the creation of this book. To my family, friends, and spiritual mentors, thank you for your unwavering support and prayers that sustained me in this endeavor. To the countless individuals whose stories of triumph and faith inspired this work, I am humbled by your courage and resilience. Finally, to my readers, thank you for embarking on this journey with me. May your lives be enriched by the truths shared within these pages.

MATTERS OF THE HEART: THE HEALING GOD (4TH EDITION

THE END

About the Author

Patience Sakutukwa is a true Renaissance woman, seamlessly blending her entrepreneurial prowess with her deep spiritual commitment. Her multifaceted roles as an author, CEO, theologian, mentor, and advocate underscore her dedication to both personal growth and societal impact. Through her literary works like "Matters of the Heart" and her leadership at Bethel Publishing House, she's not only sharing her insights but also empowering others to explore the depths of their faith and relationships.

www.ingramcontent.com/pod-product-compliance
Lightning Source LLC
Chambersburg PA
CBHW060649030426
42337CB00017B/2520